FAMOUS PEOPLE GREAT EVENTS

Florence Nightingale

by Emma Fischel
Illustrations by Peter Kent

W
FRANKLIN WATTS
LONDON • SYDNEY

This edition 2012

Franklin Watts
338 Euston Road
London NW1 3BH

Franklin Watts Australia
Level 17/207 Kent Street
Sydney NSW 2000

Text first published as *Famous People, Famous Lives: Florence Nightingale* in 1997

© text Emma Fischel 1997, 2012
© illustrations Peter Kent 1997, 2012

The right of Emma Fischel to be identified
as the author of this work has been asserted.

The right of Peter Kent to be identified
as the illustrator of this work has been asserted.

ISBN: 978 1 4451 0863 6

Dewey Decimal Classification Number: 610.7'3'092

A CIP catalogue record for this book
is available from the British Library.

Series editor: Sarah Peutrill
Original series editor: Sarah Ridley
Artwork: Peter Kent (line), Lisa Williams (colour)
Consultant: Dr Anne Millard

Printed in China

Franklin Watts is a division of Hachette Children's Books, an

Chapter 1

"Let's take a long trip round Europe," said Mrs Nightingale to Mr Nightingale, "like other rich people do."

By the time they got home they had had two daughters. Each was named after the city she was born in. Parthenope ... and Florence.

Parthenope

Florence

Naples, ancient city of Parthenope. 1819

Florence, 1820

The Nightingales lived in a house in Derbyshire. It was a very big house, but not big enough for Mrs Nightingale.

So they bought a bigger house in Hampshire too.

Florence had lots of toys and pets to play with – and twenty-seven cousins.

Life was very different then for girls. There was no school at all for poor girls and even rich ones weren't taught much.

Florence was, though, thanks to her father. Florence's mother was worried. "No one likes CLEVER girls!" she said.

"Piano playing, embroidery, flower arranging – that's what my daughter needs to learn!"

But Florence would grow up to do a lot more than flower arranging.

When Florence was seventeen the Nightingales went to Europe again. They visited many different places and had lots of fun.

But Florence got bored in the end. She was glad when they arrived back home. "I've had enough of parties," she said. "I'd like to study maths now, please."

Her parents didn't think much of that idea.

So Florence found something her parents WOULD let her do. She went visiting the poor and sick. She did her best to help them.

I must bring the fever down – but how?

Chapter 2

Florence wanted to learn more. "I must work in a hospital now," she said.

Even her father got cross this time – but, then, hospitals were not the same in those days.

But one person was on her side. He was a very important man called Sidney Herbert. "Nursing needs people like you," he said.

"If you really want to learn, then start with these!"

Florence took the books and studied every one of them in secret.

The more Florence read,
the more she knew she had
to try to change things.

Not many people wanted to be nurses. Nurses were often dirty old women who drank too much and robbed their patients.

Patient after patient slept in the same sheets.

Surgeons used dirty knives to operate.

Poor people were packed into overcrowded smelly hospitals. The rich were nursed at home.

Many nurses couldn't read or write. They had no training and most of their patients died.

"We shall send you abroad," said her
mother. "That will get this crazy notion of
nursing out of your head once and for all!"

But it didn't.
In fact, it did the
opposite. While
she was away
Florence found
just the place to
learn, and this
time no one was
there to stop her.

KAISERWERTH
INSTITUTION
DUSSELDORF-GERMANY
VOLUNTEER NURSES
ALWAYS WANTED

At the Kaiserwerth Institution hospital Florence got up at five every morning and worked late into the night.

When she came home three months later, she found plenty of work to do right in her own house.

As Florence nursed her sick family back to health, word was spreading about her.

Florence was asked to run a big hospital.

She quickly found that running a big hospital meant doing everything.

11

Then a horrible disease called cholera broke out.

Soon thousands of people were ill. Florence moved to a big hospital packed with cholera victims.

Her family worried about her. Cholera was very easy to catch and many people died from it.

But disease was not the only danger looming. The Crimean War was going on between Russia and Turkey. After a year, Britain and France joined in against Russia.

Soon bad news came back.

THE TIMES

14 October 1854

MORE DIE IN HOSPITAL THAN ON BATTLEFIELD

By William Howard Russell

Wounded soldiers were taken to a hosptial in a place called Scutari in Turkey, but there were no nurses there to help the doctors.

"Soldiers are dying needlessly. I must DO something," said Florence.

So Florence wrote to Sidney Herbert ...

... just as Sidney Herbert wrote to Florence. Sidney asked Florence to run the hospital at Scutari.

Chapter 3

Soon Florence and thirty-eight nurses set off for Turkey. They arrived at Scutari on the 4th November, 1854. Florence was now thirty-four years old.

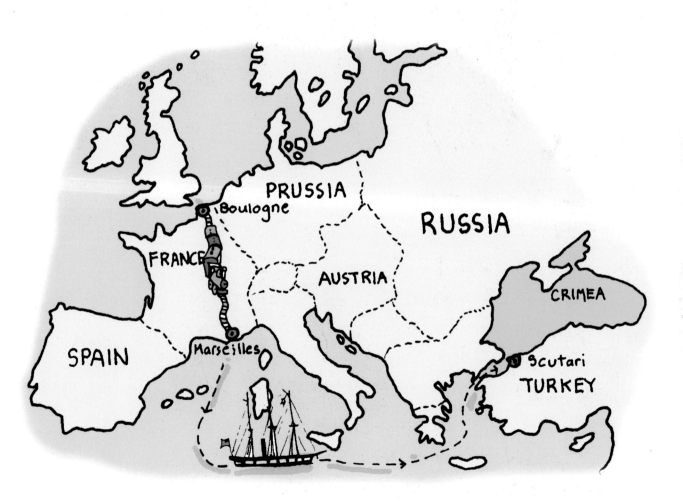

The hospital was dark and filthy. Everywhere, soldiers lay wounded and dying. More were arriving all the time.

Everything was dirty. There was hardly any clean water, no medicines, no bandages, no soap or towels.

Instead of getting better, most of the soldiers got worse.

So Florence and her nurses set to work.

Then Florence rented a house. She turned it into a laundry to clean the sheets and clothes of the soldiers. She hardly even stopped to sleep.

Every day there were new problems to sort out. What was worse, some of the doctors didn't want her there. Nor did some of the army officers.

"What does a woman know about running a hospital in wartime?" they said.

But Florence bullied and bossed and persuaded. And slowly, the hospital began to change for the better.

The wounded soldiers loved her. She did everything she could to help them get well.

She asked for books and games to be sent from England – and a chef to be sent from France.

She even wrote letters for the ones who couldn't write themselves.

And every single evening she walked through every single ward to say goodnight.

The soldiers called her the Lady with the Lamp.

Then Florence fell dangerously ill. For twelve days no one knew if she would live or die. By now, people back in England knew all about Florence and her brave work. Everyone waited anxiously for news.

When the war ended big celebrations were planned to welcome her home.

But Florence didn't want a fuss, so she fooled them all.

Chapter 4

Queen Victoria invited Florence to stay with her in Scotland.

Florence told the Queen all about the horrors of Scutari. "And it will happen again if we don't do something to change things," she said.

Then Florence showed the Queen a few ideas she had. "We are most impressed with her knowledge and, err, thoroughness," said the Queen.

It wasn't just the army that Florence wanted to change.

She visited workhouses, where the poorest people lived.

WORKHOUSE

How often do the children have fresh fruit?

Christmas Day, ma'am. One plum each.

She went round slums, where houses were crowded together and diseases spread fast.

She tried to work out what was wrong, and then find ways to make things better.

She spent a lot of time telling important people what needed doing – even if they didn't always want to listen.

And, bit by bit, she got things done.

Chapter 5

Sidney Herbert was worried about Florence. "You're doing too much," he said.

"Not enough, Sidney!" said Florence. "And now I have a few ideas about India!"

Although India was far away, it was ruled by the British then. People died in their millions from diseases and hunger.

Florence wrote letters to doctors all over India. She asked them lots of questions.

And she received lots of answers.

The answers went into a report on the problems in India. It was two thousand pages long.

Florence was ill a lot between the ages of forty and sixty. But even being stuck in bed didn't stop her working – although her cats sometimes did.

A training school for nurses was set up and named after her. The students lived in the hospital while they trained.

Florence was very kind to the students. She held tea parties for them and even paid for them to go on holiday.

When Florence was eighty, her eyesight got so bad she had to stop working. That same year Queen Victoria died.

The new king, Edward VII, gave Florence a very special honour, called the Order of Merit. It was the first time it had ever been given to a woman.

Florence died when she was ninety. Everyone wanted to give her a big public funeral in Westminster Abbey.

But Florence had told them not to make a fuss.

FN

Born 1820

Died 1910

Further facts

Doctors and nurses

The first British woman who became a doctor had to go to America and Switzerland to study medicine. Only men were allowed in British universities.

The Nightingale Training School showed that there was more to nursing than changing sheets and feeding patients. For the first time nurses wore uniforms and took exams.

Sights and smells

Some of Florence's improvements were very simple, like opening hospital windows! Many people thought fresh air spread diseases so the windows were often boarded up at the start of winter.

A lot of hospitals had no lavatories, just chamber pots under the beds. They were filled a lot – but not emptied half as much.

Florence brought in screens to put round beds in her hospitals. Before that, most operations were done in full view of all the other patients.

Some important dates in Florence Nightingale's lifetime

1820 Florence is born on 12th May, in Florence, Italy.

1837 Victoria becomes Queen of England. Florence goes on a tour of Europe.

1851 Florence works for three months at Kaiserwerth, in Dusseldorf, Germany.

1853 Florence runs her first hospital in Harley Street, London.

1854 The Crimean War begins. In November Florence goes to Scutari in Turkey, to work at the army hospital.

1855 Florence is dangerously ill but recovers.

1856 War ends. Florence returns to England and meets Queen Victoria.

1860 The Nightingale Training School for nurses opens in London.

1901 Queen Victoria dies.

1907 Florence is given the Order of Merit.

1910 Florence dies on 13th August.

Quiz

Can you remember?

1. What was Florence named after?

2. Who taught Florence?

3. What did Florence do as she wasn't allowed to study maths?

4. Who encouraged Florence to be a nurse?

5. When did Florence get the chance to work as a nurse?

6. What disease made thousands of people ill while Florence was running her first hospital?

7. When did Florence go to Turkey to nurse wounded soldiers?

8. What was wrong with the hospital in Turkey?

9. What did the soldiers call Florence and why?

10. What country did Florence write a report on?

11. What did King Edward VII give to Florence?

12. How old was Florence when she died?

Answers on page 32

Glossary

Chamber pot A bowl kept in a bedroom and used as a toilet, especially at night.

Cholera An infectious and often deadly disease that causes severe vomiting and diarrhoea.

Disease An illness. Some diseases can be caught from other people and some cannot.

Dressing A medical covering for a wound, usually made of cloth.

Embroidery Sewing patterns and pictures on to fabric.

Order of Merit An award given to someone for remarkable service in the armed forces, science, art or literature.

Persuade To make someone do what you want or agree with you.

Slum A lot of crowded, run-down houses.

Surgeon A doctor who uses tools to work on a patient's body.

Workhouse A building where poor people could work for food and shelter.

Index

Quiz answers

1. The city she was born in
2. Her father
3. Visited the poor and the sick
4. Sidney Herbert
5. When her mother sent her abroad
6. Cholera
7. 1854
8. Everything was dirty, no clean water, medicine, bandages, towels etc
9. The Lady with the Lamp because she walked through the hospital every night saying goodnight to the soldiers
10. India
11. The Order of Merit
12. 90